No More Wars, Please

My Journey from Lebanon to America

No More Wars, Please

My Journey from Lebanon to America

Alexandre Hageboutros, MD

iUniverse, Inc.
New York   Bloomington

No More Wars, Please
My Journey from Lebanon to America

iUniverse books may be ordered through booksellers or by contacting:

iUniverse
1663 Liberty Drive
Bloomington, IN 47403
www.iuniverse.com
1-800-Authors (1-800-288-4677)

ISBN: 978-0-595-50845-7 (sc)
ISBN: 978-0-595-50101-4 (dj)
ISBN: 978-0-595-61674-9 (ebook)

Printed in the United States of America

iUniverse rev. date: 2/27/2009

This book is dedicated to my wife, Ghada; my precious daughters, Karine and Joelle; my father, Daniel; and my mother, Gilberte.

Contents

Scars of War
Lebanon
My neighborhood, Ain El Remaneh, June 1981

CHAPTER I   The Nightmare

I woke up scared and shaky; I had had a nightmare. I was six years old and I still remember. It was 1968. I was alone, wandering in my neighborhood. The street was quiet, but the silence was unusual for that street in broad daylight. No one was near, and suddenly I thought I heard wailing; then a terrified face appeared. The dream became more and more intense. As I looked at the once bustling street, I realized something was wrong, but what was it? I could not wake up. I knew I was dreaming and I wanted the dream to end. The voices became more forceful when the distant echoes became closer and the faces more frightening. By now I was running. There was still no one around, but a face spontaneously appeared in the windows of the deserted apartment rooms of the towering buildings lining the street. The color of the buildings, the street, and the trees were all grayish-brown. I don't know how long it lasted, but when I finally woke up, I had an eerie feeling, a kind of premonition of impending doom.

Ten years later, in 1978, I came back to that street in the suburbs of Beirut; it was desolate in broad daylight. I heard screams and wailing. I was a rescuer with the Red Cross team responding to a distress call. A bombshell had just fallen close to the front of the building. Gray and brown smoke filled the air. The silence was only interrupted by sounds of explosives and screaming children.

When I arrived with my team at the scene, a man wearing a suit was lying on the floor. His face was gray mixed with red. We checked the man; he did not move. I had never seen a dead man before.

I was born in Lebanon. I grew up in Furn el Chebback, one of the suburbs of Beirut. School was a fifteen-minute walk from home. I would cross Damascus Street, a busy highway, dodging cars, bikes, and trucks. This would give me the adrenaline rush to start my day. I would then walk leisurely along a narrow street, flanked by buildings two to three stories high, passing the bookstore of my second grade teacher on the left, the house of my friend on the right, and a few stores on both sides of the streets selling colorful fruits and vegetables displayed in small boxes. At the end of that road, I would make a right turn onto a steep way leading to my elementary school of College de Notre Dame. My school was run by the Brothers of La Salle. At the school's entrance was a large, metallic gray door, with a golden star in the middle. Once I passed the gate, the school church was a few steps ahead. It was a long, white, rectangular structure, with an arched roof and tinted glass windows. A long staircase led to its entrance. Underneath the church were a basketball court and the restrooms. To the right was the playground, including a basketball and several volleyball courts, shaded by big trees. The track and soccer field started where the church ended. The lower school, to the right of the soccer field, had two small stores that opened during recess and sold candies only.

We started gathering under the church, sometimes playing a game of marbles until the bell rang. We would then gather in two straight rows under the church according to our class and head teacher. The vice principal of the school, Monsieur Antoine, would then appear at the top of the staircase. His appearance was always followed by a moment of silence. *"Distance!"* the headmaster would yell, and we would distance ourselves one arm's length from the person in front of us. Then came the marching order, class by class. We went to our classrooms. We would always stand up in class when anyone would visit our classroom. The only time we stepped out of our classroom was for gym, art, recess, or punishment.

Punishment for disturbing the peace in the classroom was rarely physical. Writing an apologetic sentence a few hundred times was more common. But the worst was to be sent to the office of the vice principal, Monsieur Antoine. There were rumors circulating of a dungeon with all kinds of insects and rodents, but no one was ever sent there.

At recess, we played several games, like volleyball, dodge ball, basketball, or marbles, which was my favorite game because I could sometimes go home with some extra marbles. There were also fights. I remember once in first grade, one of my classmates with whom I had an argument threw a small rock that nearly hit my left eye and left me with a scar I still bear on my left eyebrow today.

I dreaded the yearly physically exam. The other boys were always spreading rumors of needle injections and other tortures that never occurred. The most memorable moment was the last day of school, when the awards were delivered to the best in class. I had to wait until the fifth grade to hear my name called, as I received my first award for French, Math, and Science. It was also the last year of peacetime; it was the summer of 1974.

Peace came to an abrupt end one Sunday afternoon on April 13, 1975. It was the first time I heard gun shots. I remember this moment vividly. Instead of hiding, my father and I went out to our balcony to check out what had happened. I saw people on the street running and yelling, and others gathering and pointing in the direction of the source of gun fire.

I did not understand what was happening. My father probably knew the gravity of the event. I could see it in his eyes, but he reassured me. The shelling of residential areas started during the spring of 1975. It was good news to hear the whistle of death because it meant the bomb had passed above our heads, making a sound like a whistle before exploding a few seconds later. It was also bad news because it meant that somebody else got hurt.

Years went by from 1975 to 1985, and grown-ups kept saying, "Another forty-eight hours and this nightmare will end." I remember growing up in an environment where collecting bullets and unexploded mortar shells was more fashionable than collecting stamps. The extremes were the ear collectors. I could not believe it until a young man showed me a jar full of them. I did not ask who they belonged to; I was nauseated enough to cut the discussion short. I had to live, grow up, and mature in this environment. I had no other choice. Other people's irreconcilable differences were imposed on my life, shaping it. What was it all about? I still cannot figure it out. Action and reaction lead to a disastrous, never-ending war.

You tend to get used to both war and peacetime. Both were scary. War was scary for its obvious reasons but also because you may not see its end. Peace was scary because it was precarious. It was like an intense reminder of life and death; you didn't know when it would start or when it would end. God blessed us with a short-term memory; we have a tendency to forget the war when it is peacetime. Those who had to know when it would start or end wasted their lives waiting rather than living; they were innocent prisoners who served time, waiting.

My father probably saved my life by always insisting that I stay away from political parties, which required that members join the armed militia. I had to help my people, so I joined the Lebanese Red Cross when I was seventeen, not realizing that it was at the time more dangerous than being in the trenches.

I thought I could not get hurt—typical adolescent thinking. A bombshell blew up a gas tank one morning, sending loud noises across town. The building was on fire. Women and children were stuck on the fourth floor of the inferno building.

I was among the first rescue team to get to the scene. I went upstairs; smoke was starting to fill the air. My teammate needed another rescue box, which we had left in the ambulance. Without any delay or thought of danger, I went down the steps from the fourth floor, when suddenly smoke filled the air. Two seconds later, I could not see my way.

I held onto the wall, and step by step, I went to the third floor. I turned right onto the steps leading to the lower level. It was probably less than a second. Today I feel it still, like an eternity. What I thought was the steps of the staircase that would lead me to the lobby of the building was in fact the elevator cage, left wide open by the explosion.

My left foot miscalculated; my right foot followed. It was a free fall into an image of hell; a wild fire was burning at the garage level of the elevator. I saw all this in a split second. The smoke was thick and dark, and the oxygen was scarce.

I had no time to think. My right hand grabbed the edge of the floor at the opening where I fell. With a strong will to live, surmounted by a feeling that my time had not yet come, I grabbed hold of something with my left hand, which I later realized was a cable. With no one else there to help me, every muscle was mobilized in one single lifesaving effort, lifting me up back to where I started my free fall. I was able to locate the staircase and take every step down the staircase, crawling as the smoke intensified. The visibility was poor and the oxygen was scarce. I raced carefully down to the lobby of the building and had to be helped by the people I was supposed to rescue.

I coughed black smoke particles for two weeks after. Each time I think back, a chill runs down my spine. I was and still am convinced that a guardian angel was looking after me, and on that day he lent me his hand, which I grabbed with my left hand. I rationalize it now, trying to explain how, in a split second, my life could have ended; my scientific mind only saw the cable hanging from the elevator, which may have been stuck on the fourth or fifth level. It was a coincidence maybe, or a perfect alignment of my extended arm and the cable, with no room for error, that I grabbed the cable. Nevertheless, that's what I believe came to my rescue. It was there for me to grab, but I did not see it or know it existed. I did not rationalize then; it was a divine hand that helped me. I knew then that God existed. I was raised in the Catholic faith and learned that God is good and present everywhere, but I asked myself, *If God is love, how could he allow such suffering, injustice, and hatred? Does God really love us or are we just part of an experiment in freedom? Why should I pay the price for other people's bad choice?*

Could we be living in hell now? It is a question that did not cross my mind then. I believed then that heaven and hell were only part of what could happen in the future, not now, in the present. I believe there is a beginning and an end to life; therefore, there must be a creator whose scheme is not always clear to us. My line of questioning has to stop somewhere. I have to move on and see what will happen or else I will get lost in resolving a question that no one but the Creator can answer.

For some of us, the Bible is the closest thing we have to an instruction manual that comes with our life. So many people fought over the interpretation of this book that the message is not very clear. Everyone seems to have a different understanding of the message. Some live by the book; some rule by the book.

Are we alone in this journey or do we have a guide? Who is our guide, the book of words or the words of the book? There are always two choices in life: life or death, truth or lie, left or right. Most of the time, we do not see it as clearly as we see black and white. Even with black or white, there are shades of gray. We always have to choose one answer, one way, one life.

My next mission, in the spring of 1981, was a rescue and relief effort to Zahle, a town besieged by the Syrian Army for its beliefs. It was a symbol of the Lebanese resistance to the occupation as well as a strategic location close to the main road between Damascus and Beirut. On the morning of April 2, 1981, my convoy left the Red Cross headquarters in Beirut for Zahle.

I proudly wore my big cross across my chest; it was red. I went through towns I had never seen. I came across people I had never met, with fear in their eyes and hate in their hearts. Our convoy took a scenic drive through the beautiful mountains of my country. I realized this day that my roots were there; this was my land, which no one could deny. I was torn between pride and shame; I could not protect my roots. We made a turn, and beyond the mountain laid a fertile valley, the Bekaa Valley.

The convoy stopped. Negotiations were taking place. I looked around to the place I used to come with my parents and eat the tastiest *labneh* sandwiches I ever ate. *Labneh* is softer than cream cheese and made of plain yogurt that is left to dry in a cloth bag. The *markouk* bread is a sort of pita bread as thin as a page of this book, which is tossed on a dome-shaped heated stone with a few leaves of mint and a few olives; this rolled sandwich brought a cascade of memory flashes of fresh mountain air and beautiful fertile valley rushing in with every bite—memories of the past and visions of the future. The taste was different now, sourer than ever, and the future was more uncertain. The air was gray, and the people wore green and brown uniforms. They were not the same people I encountered when I was a child visiting this town. These people robbed my land.

We finally made our approach to the besieged town of Zahle; it first appeared to be a ghost town, filled with broken glass, open doors, and the bleeding wounded who were about to die. Our next stop was the center of this once bustling town. The hospital was filled with war casualties and sick people. The sick wanted to leave so their illness would not burden the fight for freedom. They were proud and fearless.

The convoy was on the way back. I was sitting in the back of the ambulance with five wounded civilians. Suddenly, the convoy stopped. We heard yelling and cursing. Men in green were inspecting the content of the convoy. Suddenly, without warning, one of them opened the back door of the ambulance. He pointed a gun at me, asked for my name, and wanted to know who these people were. He was ready to shoot.

Some people are trained to react rather than think, like a machine; you push the wrong button and suddenly you are dead.

These people don't come with an instruction manual. They are as unpredictable as life is. Even if there was an instruction manual, like a Bible for example, everyone would interpret it differently, even the killing machine itself.

As I was thinking of how to answer him, one of the sick coughed several times. The response suddenly occurred to me: "I am who I am, but this man is very sick. He has tuberculosis." The man in green turned green. I could see fear in his eyes, and his hand was shaking. He did not ask more. He quickly closed the door and ordered us to speed away. I learned that day that words are the ultimate weapon. That day, I believe I decided I wanted to be a doctor. One of man's worst fears is his health. He worries about it more than his life. I did not know that much about tuberculosis then, nor did the man who coughed; he probably had the flu. The convoy made it home safely, but the war went on.

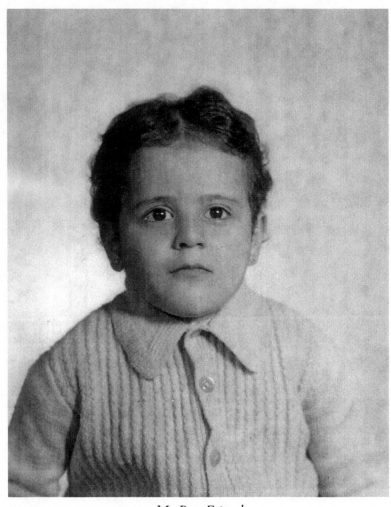

My Best Friend
1965

CHAPTER II My wife, my life

On September 1, 1980, I was admitted into the Saint Joseph University medical school in Beirut, directed by French Jesuits priests. The power to heal and the respect of others were the main attractions; and at that time, I thought education was definitely the ticket out of this chaos.

I was accepted into three medical schools: Saint Joseph University on the eastern side of Beirut, the American University of Beirut on the western side, and the University of Bordeaux in France; the choice was shaped by the political climate and the war that was fueling this stormy climate.

Saint Joseph University was located in the most dangerous part of Beirut, within a few blocks of the line of fire that divided the city at that time. I had to choose between being in the line of fire or the risk of being kidnapped by crossing to the western side of town or leaving the country all together. It gave a totally different meaning to the phrase "safety college" used in America.

I don't know whether I'd be writing now or even if I'd still be alive had I made a different choice. So many things would have changed for better or for worse. Blessed is this choice of university that put me in the path of the woman of my life. I met Ghada on the first day of class. She was wearing a yellow shirt and a blue skirt. We had just entered the classroom; she turned around and asked me my name. I did not know then that she would be my wife. The present was pleasant, the future did not matter, and the past did not exist. We later crossed ocean and sea, survived war and earthquake, together. She was born the same year as I, in the same town. She has four sisters. She also saw the same ugly face of the war. When the fighting was intense, she used to find cover in a shelter nearby. One dreadful night, bombs were falling all around, and suddenly a cloud of smoke followed a loud sound. When the dust settled, she found her eighteen-year-old neighbor, who had been sitting next to her, immobile on the floor. The woman was unconscious, but when she awoke and her mind cleared, her legs remained paralyzed. It was a rude awakening to the reality of war. This was the experience of adolescence, a shocking introduction to the reality of adulthood.

Ghada's best memories of her childhood were the few summer vacations to Roum, the mountain village of her father. The anticipation was great; the preparations for the trip were no less exciting. I visited her summerhouse with our daughters, Karine and Joelle, when we visited her parents a few years back. The once proud owner had to ask permission to visit her own playground, her own room. It is now occupied, like the rest of the land, by a bunch of strangers who found refuge in empty homes. She was nonetheless proud to show us her house, with a balcony that overlooked a beautiful garden with a majestic view of the valley. Her father told me many times about the work he had done on this house, from the modern electrical system to foundation reinforcement to resist any earthquake. In the village, a few veterans who never left recognized the little girl in her.

My summerhouse did not have a better fate; it was destroyed by a government project to build a highway. She visited my childhood haven before it was reduced to rubble.

We built our relationship on friendship. One of Ghada's fa-vorite quotes was "A friendship that ends never started." We grew up together, listening, learning, and helping each other. Countless times, we both thought the same thing at the same time. We would even say the same words to express an idea that just crossed our minds. It is as if we communicated at a different level, as if our mouths were echoing what our minds were discussing.

We studied together. She challenged me to excel, and I owe it to her that my rank in class skyrocketed from sixty-seventh to seventh within a year. We spent long hours studying in her room, in daylight or sometimes in candlelight. Her aunt would make us delicious grilled feta cheese sandwiches. Her mother would cook us dinner. Her sister would get us sweets. We were spoiled; all we had to do is study.

I taught her to drive in my rusty, old, white Alfasud. She had a blue Renault 5. The breaks of the Alfasud were beyond repair. One day, I was in a hurry to get to her house, and a car in front of me stopped suddenly; it also helped to stop mine. Another day, she was returning home when a car stopped suddenly in front of her. She lost control, and the Renault 5 tumbled upside down, slid down a slope, and finally stopped. She came out of the car unharmed—not a scratch. Many years later, on a Christmas trip to Canada, we experienced a near-death experience driving with the whole family. The Crown Victoria we rented skated on ice in the middle of the Adirondack. I was driving in a snow storm, on cruise control—big mistake. With seven lives in the car, suddenly the waltz started. One turn and my mother interjected, "Slowly. Calm down." The second turn was getting close to the ravine. There was silence. The third turn was toward the midline division of the highway. Within ten seconds, the excitement was over. We took a deep breath. There was no damage, but the engine stalled. I had restarted the engine of this big frozen car in the middle of a freeway, once, then twice, when two lights appeared in my visor. The third time, the engine miraculously started. Within three long seconds after clearing the freeway and moving to the right lane, a long eighteen-wheeler truck flew by. The rest of the trip to Montreal took the longest and most stressful couple of hours ever.

Ghada and I became great friends. We attended the same classes in medical school and we watched movies together. She preferred the intellectual French movies that sparked our discussions, while I preferred the James Bond type of movies. She spoke to me about Camus, Sartre, DeBeauvoir, and Groult. I had never read these authors; I preferred Spirou and Tintin comic books. I was challenged by her wealth of knowledge, and I could not impress her with my knowledge of electronics, a boring subject.

Together we survived the war. We lived intense moments of fear, darkness, anxiety, and despair. We felt stuck in this inferno with no hope of a better future. This created a strong bond between us. We were two teenagers longing to live a normal life, but the circumstances decided otherwise.

One night, we were driving to the movies. All was calm. The music was on as we were discussing our future. Everything came to an abrupt stop when five drunken men crossed the highway. I had to decide in an instant whether to brake and risk losing control of the car on wet pavement or maneuver around them. I had two choices, which would have lead to two different outcomes. I chose to wiggle around them. They did not appreciate the thrill of the experience. As I looked back in my rearview mirror, I saw a man in green pulling his pistol out. He aimed and fired two shots at us. He missed. There was no respect for life; some were ready to kill at a whim. We were supposed to go to the movies, but we settled for a drink, a strawberry and banana milkshake with whipped cream. It tasted better than ever before. We always seem to appreciate life better after we face the prospect of losing it.

Long after we were married, Ghada reminded me of the day a rocket exploded in her neighbor's apartment. It was a calm evening; we were both sitting at her desk, studying for an exam, when a strident noise ruptured the moment. The glass window shattered and shrapnel flew around us. The instinctive reaction in a moment like this is self-protection, but without any hesitation, I threw my body on her as a shield, to protect her. Her life was more important to me than my own. We did not get hurt, but the energy of the bomb soldered our lives together. I must have known then that her life was as important to God as I thought mine was. She knew then there could never be any stronger proof of love than this moment.

War Games
1968, Furn El Chebback,
I pose for my brother on the balcony of my room,
playing soldier with my toy machine gun.

CHAPTER III   The War

War showed its ugly face again one afternoon in the summer of 1986. While on service in the emergency room as a medical student, I heard the sirens of ambulances. The rescuer brought to my room a seven- or eight-year-old boy who a few minutes prior was playing soccer with his friends when a bomb shattered its shrapnel on his small and innocent body. His left leg was gone, his chest was pierced, and he was holding on to his life by a thread. We could not save him. He died. I stopped hearing everything around me for an instant as if nature had a moment of silence.

I was mad. I asked why but got no answer. I thought this must be the hell that I always heard about in religious education. *But we are here, so we should make the best out of this life,* I concluded. This thought helped me survive the psychological impact of the war and shaped my view of life. The problem is and always will be that what is best for me may not be best for you. This difference of opinion is the origin of all world's conflicts.

The first option to resolve such conflicts is war; we impose our way by force. The second solution is peace with compromise; we respect each other's differences, as it was once taught some two millennia ago. Love each other; it is as simple as that.

I have thought about this since then, and I realized that it is not so simple. We also have to agree on the way to love each other. We have some individuality to preserve in this society: our self image, our thoughts, our likes and dislikes, our tastes, our morals, our ways. If we are outsiders to the game of life, we will view war as evil and peace as good. We must then be on the side of good. Somebody must be on the side of evil, from my point of view. That somebody would view me on the side of evil as he would view himself of the side of good. Who is right and who is wrong?

If everything is relative to us, then maybe the difference between good and evil does not exist. We need this analogy of good and evil to earn our individuality, to separate us from the crowd, to say that we are different. Whether we like it or not, we are all part of one world, and we are not outsiders to the game of life.

Religion and society tried the compromise card, betting on common views to attract many followers. Is there a unique umbrella that would cover us all, a unifying common view? The one who will find this unique view should be God, and the place should be heaven.

Alexander the Great, Caesar, and Napoleon were among a group of men who thought they had the answer; they imposed it on others by means of force and failed. Others will follow their footsteps and will fail again, like the many who are trying now. Why do they keep trying? Probably because they are blind and they never see the way, though they believe they do. They lead the sheep into the abyss and back again.

During the darkest moments of that war, I used to daydream. I would create my own world where I would be the one who would save my people from the grip of war. Over the years, my fantasy evolved from being a war hero who would rally his neighborhood around his leadership, to being a prince who would win the admiration of the world.

Somehow the ends of my stories were obvious, but the road to get there was always murky. I was never able to find a solution to end the war, but I never lost faith that is was possible. I could always see what it would be like to live that dream. Just to live the dream was worth it. I became an outsider on the side of good. The answer did not matter; all that mattered was the fact that it could happen.

I created in my mind the perfect leader, the perfect constitution, and the perfect world—as Jean Jacques Rousseau named it, Utopia. But it was only in my mind; I did not have the power to make it real. Great ideas must have been a dream, a kind of blue print conceived in our mind.

The time I spent in my dreams was more pleasant than the nights I spent scared of the sound and light of bombs rumbling through my neighborhood streets and slamming on my balcony.

As crazy as it sounds, I was only once really afraid of dying during those fifteen years of war. It was a Thursday afternoon. The sounds of explosions were becoming louder as the bombing was making its unpredictable entrance into my neighborhood. The Organ of Stalin was playing Mozart's *Requiem*. In French we called it *l'Orgue De Stalin,* a rocket launcher capable of simultaneously firing forty rockets. It was used by the Russians to defeat the German army in World War II. Forty loud explosions echoed forty distant sounds soon after. Then another forty followed the footsteps of destruction. Surrounded by the whistling of rockets, the shattering of windows, the fallout of shrapnel rain repeating its deadly cycle, I hoped to hear the last note of this sordid music.

I realized that I was young, too young to die. I was scared, but like everybody else, I sat in this area we called the safest room in our sixth-floor apartment. I kept silent and carefully listened to the symphony of rockets, without even coughing or clearing my throat, in respect for this moment, which could be my last. I listened to the last note and decided then to leave. Leave my country, leave my roots, and immigrate to America. I recalled this moment many years later while listening to the Philadelphia Orchestra playing Wagner's symphony. I started to focus on strengthening my command of the English language, which I only learned as a third language in high school, and looked at all the steps I needed to continue my medical education in the United

States. The Internet had not been born yet. Our university had ties to France, so I had to rely on the experience of only a few faculty members who had trained in the United States a decade or more prior.

The sounds of rifles, rockets, and other instruments of war were also now part of the celebration of peace for everyone in this conflict as it became the universal language that tied us together. We heard them in peacetime, during weddings and funerals alike, as if we missed the sound of war. Some people became addicted to the music or perhaps they wanted to experience the intense moment that separated life and death during these happy or sad times. They would fire their weapons in the air. It was insane. War and peace were alike; good and evil danced together.

One black Saturday, as it was called then in 1981, my friend Simon was kidnapped. He was a devoted rescuer with no political links, a young man with a determination to rescue even if it cost him his life. He followed a similar path to the one I had chosen, to join the rescue effort through the Red Cross, to cope with the war. The day before his abduction, a truce was in place. The next day it was madness; innocent bystanders were killed in the name of their religious identity, and for no other reason. The passage through the divided city became the passage to the holocaust. In one day, for no reason, madness prevailed; every citizen lost a loved one that day. To date, Simon's fate remains unknown.

What turned the madness of what happened in the city that day on or off? Most of the time, words rather than actions fuel the fire. It did not matter who started or who ended it. Some human behaviors are reminiscent of those of the worst predator. The atrocities committed in the name of God were countless. It was the same God but viewed from a different angle, evil or good depending on which side of the fence you were on.

I saw men dragged through my streets. I also saw them on television on my neighbors' streets, and the men dragging probably all watched the same old Western movies of people dragging men behind their horses. The men who dragged them on both sides of the screen looked alike, with their beards and green uniforms.

Despite witnessing these atrocities, we had to continue to live as normally as we could. We studied by candlelight. In the background were the sounds of explosions, the loud speakers of the mass or the distant voice from the mosque, and the sound of the electrical generators. Some nights were quiet; I sat on the balcony and watched the stars. My brother Pierre used to tell me that the star I see today had probably died; its spirit is coming to visit us and continue on its path beyond us.

Ghada and I started our internship at the military hospital in January of 1986. I still remember that morning when we heard some distant gunfire. Shortly after, we heard the siren of an ambulance rushing to the emergency room. A beautiful young woman was bleeding profusely from a gunshot wound in her belly. She was just going to work, crossing the virtual green line that divided the city. A sniper was just waiting for his random target; he fired a bullet that hit the middle of her body. She did not complain. She suffered with dignity as she watched everybody coming to her rescue. She was rushed to the operating room; she survived. Her protracted, complicated hospital course did not matter. What mattered was her survival.

During this time, two of my dear classmates disappeared one day; they were in love and planned to get married. They were found in a remote area, where they were both murdered. This had nothing to do with the war. They were both on the same side of the fence. War is everywhere it wants to be. This kind of violence is as unpredictable and merciless as the one we call war. We went to the funeral of our slain classmate Abdullah. His coffin was open, and his head was wrapped in a white turban to hide his wounds. We both felt pain; a part of us was gone. We prayed, but then life went on. We could not comprehend what was going on around us with the war. Another victim fell; there were so many. On graduation day, we dedicated our achievement to their memory. We let them have what war took away from them.

Memories are our link to the past, our guardian angels for the future. Most of us have a tendency to recall the moments that made us change the way we see our life and geared us toward the future. We seem to be moving forward. We often look backward to see if we can predict what our next step will be. We are so impatient to see this limited life unfold that we sometimes forget to enjoy the moment. I would like to think that this time is precious enough that we should enjoy every moment of this dream. Even a split second of being is a moment recorded in eternity. For those of us lucky enough to have more than a split second, life is beautiful.

One hot summer morning in 1986, I was a mile away from home, serving my call at the hospital, when I heard a loud explosion, which was followed by a column of smoke arising from my neighborhood. This day was supposed to be part of a truce, one of many over the years that abruptly changed back to war. A car bomb exploded. A young woman screamed as she was running away from the site of the explosion, her face covered with soot as tears flowed down it. She seemed to indicate that the explosion was in the vicinity of my home. I ran as fast as I could. I did not know if I would find my home, my family, and my neighbors as I had left them the day before.

As I approached my home, smoke filled the air. Ambulances were rushing in and out of the area. People were screaming. They were either afraid of what they experienced or mad at what hit them. No men in green died that day, only innocent bystanders. The cowards who placed the car bomb were on the loose, with no remorse—only the satisfaction of a mission accomplished. Everyone points fingers, but no one gets caught; no one pays for their actions, which are perpetuated again and again.

I arrived at the doorstep of my building; the floor was covered with pieces of broken glass from the windows shattered by the sound of the explosion. There was no electricity; no elevators were working. I ran upstairs to the sixth floor, climbing two steps at a time, with one question in mind: will my life change?

I finally arrived at my door. My mother was waiting. She hugged me tearfully, and I thought for a moment that the worst had happened, but then I saw my father. He asked me how I was. Everyone was in a safe place at the time of the explosion.

Many explosions like this one have torn more than one neighborhood apart through the years. After the explosion, people's lives were not the same anymore. People lost their loved ones, or worse, a part of themselves. We blame it on the war, but there was real person behind these killings. A person who probably had a mother and father to turn to. The worst part of it all is that these people think that their actions are good. The car bombers, the snipers, the kidnappers all exist. They are everywhere they need to be to spread fear, to terrorize and destroy.

They are ordinary people in peacetime and killers in wartime— one individual with two faces. They are good and evil at the same time, in the same place.

Our world is complex, although most of us try to simplify it. Good or bad, here we go again like prisoners of the same idea. We evolved as a civilization from the Stone Age to the Computer Age, yet we still think the same way. We still feel the same emotions. The game of life has the same rules; only the setting has changed.

Cradle of Civilization
Byblos, Lebanon, 1996

CHAPTER IV History Lesson

I remember barely listening to my teacher during my history lesson, not realizing that I was living history that one day will be told to my children. They will wonder, as I probably did, why they should care about what happened in the past. It was on a sunny day in the summer of 1986 that I first realized the link to the past, and all these history lessons came to life. I was wandering aimlessly through the old cobblestone streets of the city of Byblos. I reached the old port and stared at the horizon through the gateway of the oldest seaport on the Mediterranean. Through the port of Byblos, the alphabet was spread to the world a few millennia ago. Those stones are still standing today as a reminder of what was there, although they cannot tell the whole story; the alphabet that escaped through its gate kept record of history.

"History repeats itself" is such an understatement. I'll have to take you back four millennia, to the birth of a great civilization. Lebanon is centrally located along the eastern seaboard of the blue Mediterranean Sea. It is a mix of green cedars looking over a fertile valley to the east and a sea of blue to the west. The cedars stand tall and proud, protecting the strip of land that hosted generations of peaceful people always threatened by greedy neighbors, jealous of the prosperous land. The Canaan first settled in this land and began trading with the Egyptians, whose powerful empire took control of the region from 1800 BC to 1400 BC. A millennium later, with the weakening of the neighboring empires, the land of Canaan thrived as a financial empire. The Greeks gave them the name Phoenician, for their prime export of the purple dye. They established trading posts all along the Mediterranean coast. The strength of this new empire was the alphabet.

In the legend of Cadmus, a Phoenician left the land to search for his sister Europa, a Phoenician princess kidnapped by Zeus. He settled in Greece, where he taught the new Phoenician alphabet.

Assyrians looked upon this rich but militarily weak empire and imposed a price for freedom. The Phoenicians paid for their freedom with the sweat of their work rather than the blood of their sons. The greedy Assyrians demanded more, and a revolt took place. The city of Sidon was destroyed in 677 BC, and the city of Tyre capitulated after a harsh resistance in 721 BC.[1, 2]

Elissa, another princess of Phoenicia, escaped to North Africa, where she established Carthage. The legend goes that she demanded from the prince a piece of land as big as the skin of a cow. He agreed, and she ordered the skin of the cow to be cut in very fine filament that delineated a large surface that would host the city of the newfound land.

The Babylonians followed the footsteps of the Assyrians. The city of Tyre rebelled against the Babylonian ruler Nebuchadnezzar, who imposed a siege of the city that was resisted for thirteen long years, from 587-74 BC, before it capitulated and its citizens were enslaved. Today their marks are set in stone on the great rock of Nahr el Kalb. Half a millennium later, the Persians established peace in this region, which would prosper again for the next two centuries until another round of violence destroyed the ancient cities of Tripoli and Sidon after the revolt of 351 BC.

The greatest of the Greeks, Alexander the Great, met a fierce resistance in his attempt to vanquish the city of Tyre in 332 BC. Tyre was then the largest Phoenician city; it included an island located half a mile from the Mediterranean shore of Lebanon.[3] It took this great warrior, who conquered the world in no time, seven long months to conquer the stubborn city of Tyre. It used to be an island of freedom in a world of imperial dictatorship. Alexander the Great changed that forever by connecting Tyre to the mainland, while Sidon compromised with the general and was spared the infliction. Even back then, it was each man for himself and Baal for all.

The most famous Phoenician warrior was Hannibal (247–187 BC) who raised the Carthaginian Empire to a military power that spanned from northern Africa to modern Spain. The Romans, who were in constant conflict with them in what was known as the Punic Wars, finally destroyed the Carthaginian Empire a century before Christ, 146 BC.[4]

The Romans built roads and universities. The center of the culture was now Beirut. Students from all over the empire sought to study at the prestigious University of Law.

The Bible is full of praise for the Cedars of Lebanon and has more than a hundred references to the tree of God.

The Song of Songs echoes the love of God for this piece of paradise.

- "Come from Lebanon my promised bride" (Song of Solomon 4:8).
- "The scent of your garments is like the scent of Lebanon" (Song of Solomon 4:11).
- "Fountain of the garden, well of living, water streams flowing down from Lebanon" (Song of Solomon 4:15).
- "His legs are as pillars of marble, set upon sockets of fine gold: his countenance is as Lebanon, excellent as the cedars" (Song of Solomon 5:15).
- "The voice of the LORD cracks the cedars; the LORD splinters the cedars of Lebanon, Makes Lebanon leap like a calf and Sirion like a young bull" (Psalms 29).

Christ visited Lebanon; his Apostles followed in his footsteps.

The Pax Romana lasted a couple hundred years; the empire

split and Constantine converted to Christianity in the year 330. Three hundred years later, Islam stepped into the region. They drove the Byzantines out of the region. Several Christians found refuge in the mountains along the sacred valley of Kadisha.

A heavy tax was again imposed on the owners of the land by the conqueror; an attempt at revolt was met with brutal force.

The Arabs ruled the area from the year 634, bringing Islam to Lebanon and its surrounding region.

By the dawn of the first millennium, freedom of religion for the Christians was severely compromised, leading to the coming of the Crusaders. In the year 1187, the Crusaders were defeated at Hattine and were driven out of the region in 1291. The Mamelouk and then the Ottoman Turks controlled the region for the next half millennium.

In 1590, Emir Fakhr El-Dine expanded his control from the mountains of Lebanon to the Mediterranean coast. He surrounded himself with Christian and Muslim advisors. He reopened trade with Europe. The ruthless Ottomans, afraid of his popularity and open policy, exiled him and then pardoned him. His popularity and power grew stronger. He unfortunately met the fate of other great Lebanese men who wanted to build a powerful free country: he was executed.

Emir Bashir Shihab II, in a struggle to gain power, was the catalyst of a conflict that would scar the relationship between the different communities of the Lebanese mountains, the Maronite and the Druze, for years to come.[5] The international community stepped in to end the conflict and sanctioned the divorce between the different communities.

The wound widened after the 1860 massacre, when more than ten thousand Christians were slaughtered under the watchful eye of the Ottoman landlord. The end of the First World War put an end to the four-century ruthless Ottoman Empire.[6]

History repeats itself, but we have a short memory. Conflicts between Sidon and Tyre two millennia ago, and conflicts between different communities years later, have left us wandering the globe, looking for the Utopia we could have had in our beloved Lebanon.

I left the port of Byblos as the sun was setting on the horizon that day with a sense of pride but also of sorrow for having to leave this land and follow the path of my ancestors. They departed from this port not knowing where their journey would take them.

Liberty
United States, 1988

CHAPTER V Coming to America

"Enough stories of war," I said to Ghada. We decided to go to America. It was in the fall of 1986, during our pediatric rotation at the main teaching hospital, Hotel Dieu de France. We had decided to get married and have children. We looked at some of the patients on the pediatric ward. We saw a number of them who were scarred by the war. It gave us even more reason to find a safer place to raise our children in the future. We studied day and night and passed our final exams to graduate as medical doctors. We got married one summer afternoon in July of 1987. She was twenty-four years old, and I had just turned twenty-five.

The same priest had blessed the wedding of my parents some three or four decades ago. The church was a lovely old stone church, with arcades and colored glass windows. My best friend Jean-Marie decorated the church with beautiful flowers that we handpicked the day before. Ghada borrowed the wedding gown from her cousin and chose my suit. Even now she is the one who buys all my clothes, a task I'm happy to relegate to her.

We got to the door of the church, with my nephew Philippe holding the rings on a white pillow. We were ready, but there was one thing missing: the music. The instrument was there, but the musician was absent. I improvised; I hummed the music that only my wife could hear. The sermon was long. The blessing concluded the ceremony. Congratulations were followed by the cutting of the cake. Two days later, I left for my new life in America. Ghada followed me shortly after.

I came to America by plane; my uncle George was waiting for me in Los Angeles's airport. I was apprehensive of the customs checkpoint. There were innumerable long lines, with people of every race standing there waiting to cross the yellow line, holding their colorful passports, speaking so many languages. Some lines moved fast while others were rather slow. There was no point moving from one line to another. This might have looked suspicious. I had seen too many movies, and the worst case scenario played in my mind. Some customs officers were probing their customer so intensely, I got the impression that my turn would come next and I might be sent back because of a question I did not answer right or a potential hesitation in my voice.

All this internal frenzy was a result of war and the checkpoint mentality. This mind-set had been fueled by the questions the men in green had asked me years ago. Questions like "Where do you come from?" or "What is your religion?" might send you to the other world if your accent was wrong or your voice was trembling. Some of these checkpoints were predictable; others came from nowhere, kind of a surprise visit. Whether the checkpoint was friendly or not, the fear was there and the adrenaline was always rushing.

My turn was coming, when suddenly a new officer arrived; he took over my line. When my turn came, I never forgot his words: "Welcome home, sir." Three words so sweet that I thought I was dreaming; it took a few seconds to realize it was real. My new life was about to start on a good foot. My uncle George was waiting for me.

I had two goals in my first few weeks in America. I had to establish myself in this new homeland. I sent three hundred applications to residency programs across the country in hopes of getting a handful of interviews that would allow me to start a residency program. The other goal was to build a home for my newly founded family.

The family is the most precious concept we cherish. In good times and bad times, in sickness and in health, family is always there. It is a gift of God, as good as life itself. We take it for granted, we rip it apart, and we even hate it sometimes. We tend to forget this gift, taken for granted as life itself; we live our time as if it was a race. We escape one family unit to build our own in the hopes of building a better one.

But there is joy in life, moments of happiness too short to appreciate. Nothing is black or white, but a mix of both makes life so complete. If there were a life where everything is black or everything is white, we might wish we had a little of both, never satisfied with what we have. We always want to be perfect, in the image of our God; life is a gift for which we just have to be thankful. What about all the misery around the world, children that live only to suffer and then die? Did they see the brighter side of life?

If we had not existed, then in our eyes, God wouldn't have, either. Do we only exist to acknowledge a God that only a few have pretended to communicate directly with, a God we have never seen, heard, or felt? I believe in God because I can only find one explanation for my creation and that of the world that surrounds me. Did God really think for one fraction of a second about me? He must have if he created me, or are we the fruit of nature, a fortuitous occurrence?

Did God create nature and then stop creating just to watch the story of the world unfold like we watch a movie? Being the creator of the movie, he must know the beginning and the end. In giving us freedom, he left it up to us to come up with the story. We must have made him so mad that he exiled us to a small spot in the middle of nowhere, called Earth. If we made him mad then maybe he thinks like us, feels like us, sees like us. After all, he created us in his image.

Good and evil must be the creation of the same God, to allow us the freedom to choose. There is another level of thinking that is beyond our understanding, which characterizes our God. We are only human.

Meanwhile, in September 1987, I was looking for a job. I found this ad in the *Los Angeles Times* that took me to an interview in a gift shop on Rodeo Drive, in Beverly Hills. I traveled there by bus. The place was *très chic* as I would say in French. A middle-aged man took me in the back of the store for my interview. When I had to tell him about my work history, I discussed my mom's china cabinet, which got hit during the war by shrapnel that ripped through the wooden cabinet, leaving the china intact. I knew about Christofle silverware and Baccarat and Lalique crystal, names that my mother taught me when I once browsed through her china cabinet. I also told him about my French language and culture.

The experienced interviewer noticed very soon that I was without real experience in his business but went on with the interview and finished with the classic, polite words, "I will call you," which usually mean, "You better find another job." The Beverly Hills experience was worth the bus ride.

A week after the interview, Ghada and I bought two bikes at a garage sale in Culver City for ten dollars. We used to bike to Marina Del Rey and also hang out at Venice Beach; we were mesmerized by the colorful display of the street merchants, the dancing roller skaters, the bodybuilders, and the curious crowd that filled the street. We settled for a slice of pizza and a pair of cheap sunglasses. The ocean was too cold to swim in, and with *Jaws* still fresh in our minds, it did not seem cool to end our lives inside a Californian shark's gut.

We woke up one morning in October of 1987, both looking at each other shaking like a leaf. We heard a rumble; that's when we realized it was the big earthquake. Run for your life! We both felt that after we escaped fifteen years of war, to die here in a natural disaster was too much to bear.

By that time, the interviews for the residency had started to come. There was a clear message: all the residency interviews were on the East Coast. We decided to move from Los Angeles to Baltimore.

The first day of December 1987, I arrived on the East Coast, and a snowstorm paralyzed the area. We settled in Towsen, Maryland, with the help of two good friends. I was able to finally rent our first apartment. That same day, I walked for miles from one car dealer to another and bought a Red Volkswagen Rabbit, a bit rusted but drivable. We bought our first piece of furniture, a mattress, at Montgomery Ward; it was on clearance. We strapped it to the roof of the red car and drove home with it.

I was working four jobs, one of which was doing pizza delivery for an unknown pizza place. The manager was a high school kid. My co-worker had told me he was a minister, a poor one without a church, an expensive commodity. I had also met the owner of the place, whom I first thought was another delivery guy in training but then found out that he was there to try to understand why his business was not successful. I was busy with my interviews, more eager to secure a real future than to deliver pizza in a shady neighborhood. After taking so many days off, I got fired for first time in my life, and it felt good. Two weeks later, the pizza place closed. It went bankrupt.

My second job was as a cashier overnight at a gas station. I later learned that my predecessor was held up one night at gunpoint. I felt safer during the war.

My third job was doing inventory for a company. These people were clicking on their counters at high speed, and I could not keep up with the pace for more than two months.

My fourth job brought me to a sad realization about society. I worked at a shelter for abused children; the manager was a wonderful, dedicated nun. I took care of these children with all my heart. These children were unhappy. It was sad to see them, knowing what they went through and that they didn't have a warm, loving home to go to. This was not God's fault; this was simply the doings of evil men. How someone could harm his own children is beyond comprehension. These kids needed all the protection and love one could give them; they were so vulnerable, so bittersweet.

On our first Christmas together, in 1987, Ghada and I had a mattress on the floor, a folding table, and three chairs. My gift was a pair of matching mugs of Mr. and Mrs. Claus that said "Our first Christmas together" and a black-and-white TV. The TV was advertised in a local paper; I called and got directions from the seller. When I got there, it was dark. The man showed me a small TV. I negotiated for the price of fifteen dollars.

We did not know at that time that we would each get a residency position and a good-paying job. We enjoyed this moment and cherished the memory of that time. This moment made us feel so rich; we always look back on it, and even today we appreciate the gift of that first Christmas in our new home.

By springtime of 1988, life took a new turn. I was at work when Ghada called me to tell me that we had received a telegram from the University of Medicine and Dentistry of New Jersey, in New Brunswick. The telegram's first words were "We are sorry." The rest told us that someone at the university made a mistake, a clerical error that would shape our future.

We had participated in a national residency matching program that matched training programs with a list of candidates. Everyone was therefore legally bound by the results of the matching. The telegram came in a day before the results were scheduled to be announced. It explained that a clerical error was made, listing six more positions than their budget permitted, and we were among those six. There was no time to waste. We hopped in the red Volkswagen Rabbit and headed to the university up north. We got there by 5:00 AM and waited until 7:00 AM to speak with the program director and the chief of the department of medicine, who were very apologetic.

We had to find a program to sponsor both of us before the results were to be released at noon; otherwise a whole year would be wasted. Our fate took us to the city of Camden in South Jersey, home of the Campbell Soup Company. Cooper Hospital was the sister institution in Camden, which happened to have two unfilled position in their residency program that year.

I still remember today our first encounter with Dr. Edward Viner, the chief of the Department of Medicine at Cooper Hospital. His decision to accept us into the program without knowing much about us has shaped our lives since. We sat in his office, trying to impress him the best we could, speaking a language that was not ours. I think he saw us beyond all those barriers.

To this day, twenty years later, Ghada and I have not missed an opportunity to thank Dr. Viner for his decision at that time and for all the support he provided us throughout the years. In turn, he himself likes to tell the story about the mistake the sister institution made by not taking us and how lucky he was to benefit from a clerical error that put us in his path.

That is how we both got a job in the same hospital; fate does good things sometimes. "La takraho charran laalho khayran" is a Lebanese proverb that means "Do not hate an evil thing; it might be for a good reason."

I said my farewells to the children I cared for and good luck to the staff that supported me. The next day, a beautiful fruit basket landed on my doorstep with similar wishes from the dedicated staff of the Saint Vincent shelter for abused children.

We packed for the city of Camden, with our mattress back on the roof of the red car. It was quite a scene on the freeway when the mattress started to fly over the roof like a magic carpet. The scene was a bit scary when viewed from the driver's seat. We finally stopped and strapped the magic mattress with nylon rope; the rest of the trip was uneventful.

We were two of the first foreign graduate interns ever to set foot in this hospital. A big challenge was ahead of us. We had to compete with local graduates who knew the system firsthand.

The tasks were multiple. First we had to learn to speak fluently a language that was not ours, and with a minimal accent to better communicate. We had to learn slang expressions, which sometimes led to hilarious comments as we did not understand the other meaning of the words. The crazy sequences of letters were as hilarious. Once a patient had a CABG, pronounced cabbage, in 1975; who cares if he ate a cabbage in 1975? What it really meant was a coronary arterial bypass graft. There was a whole new world to adapt to; the war had prepared us for the challenge.

It took a month to learn all this and to start to gain ground with closing the cultural gap between the foreigners and the natives. My challenge was tough because I started first. Our program director at that time, Dr. Stephen Gluckman, had helped us a lot in acquiring the necessary skills to survive in this new medical environment.

Ghada's immigration status was approved, but she had to wait for her visa number to come; it could take at least one more year. This was an even greater challenge for her since she was not allowed to start her residency before she received her green card. She did not give up and stay home; she instead attended the residents' conferences and impressed Dr. Edward Viner, the chief of medicine, with her breadth of knowledge, which was clearly above average. She showed so much compassion to a patient who she was only allowed to talk to; he did not understand the concept of waiting for a piece of paper for Ghada to be his doctor.

On one Saturday morning after a long night on call, I was awakened by Ghada's cry of joy. She received a letter from the INS awarding her a work permit that would allow her to start her residency immediately.

By the end of the first year we were considered to be among the most knowledgeable residents. We hit a home run, as my colleagues would say.

We introduced two graduates from our university, Philippe and Christina, to Dr. Stephen Gluckman, who accepted them into the program based on our recommendation. They also left a great impression, which opened the door in turn for Karam, Hala, Gracia, Carla, and many others—more than forty graduates from our university over the past twenty years. This is one of our best accomplishments in this friendly new land of opportunity that values people for who they are rather than where they come from.

The first year of our internship went without major events; the most memorable part was the green card. The best part about the green card was that we had to go to Greece to get it since the United States Embassy in Beirut was still closed after a car bomb destroyed its building in 1982. Our first vacation on the Greek islands was fabulous. The blue and white colors blending with the Mediterranean Sea and sun left an indelible impression of peace and beauty.

We landed at the airport; the chaos reminded us of our homeland, and we were back in the Middle Eastern culture. We stayed at the Athenea Hotel. The next morning, we took a ferry to Hydra, and we loved the island and decided to sleep in a very small hotel in the harbor.

Before the interview for the green card, Ghada went through a rigorous physical exam at a Greek clinic. The interview went well, but it was nerve-racking until we got the papers in our hand. The vacation started then, with a trip to Skiatos by plane. A bit scary I would say, since the plane landed on the runway quite abruptly and came to a stop just at the end of the runway, one foot away from the water.

We had a room with a harbor view and a red Vespa for transportation. The Vespa was a lot of fun. We drove to Koukounaris Beach, where we learned to water ski. We dined out at a restaurant in the harbor, eating tzatziki and calamari.

Vacations are a necessity of life. Everyone has a different view of the subject. Some want it to be perfect, whatever that means, while others like it to be unpredictable. Vacations should be a perfect time to live for the pleasure of living; not a must do, must eat, or must buy, but rather, there should be no words to define the moment.

Picture yourself on a sandy beach, on a warm sunny day, eating a sweet and cold watermelon, staring at a sea of blue water with a million reflections of the sun dancing to the sound of the waves, echoing the music of life that started somewhere on the horizon where the sea meets the sky in one blue shade. Life is talking to you; just listen to what it has to say. Vacation is a time to broaden our horizons, and it was a time to bring back the memories of the trips I took when I was still in Lebanon. I remembered my last visit to Venice. I was seventeen then. My aunt Sylvie lived in Mestre, about fifteen minutes from the capital of romance. My guide was my cousin Piera; Venice was more beautiful and mysterious than ever before. This was my fourth visit to the city.

My brother asked me to get the book of the *mostre,* or the international exhibition of photos. I took the vaporetto from Piazza de Roma to Piazza San Marco, with a thousand other tourists all wanting the same thing: just to walk the city in the footsteps of so many people before them—people who built, lived in, or just came to visit the marvelous city. People who wondered what it was like before, some who thought about what it might become, and a handful of people who were just living in the moment.

I will always remember another trip: I took the train to Menton on the French Riviera, where my godmother was expecting me. I always called her *Marraine,* which is "godmother" in French. She was my mother's best friend and the best godmother anyone could wish for. She did not have children. She used to live on the fifth floor of our building until the war broke out.

She immigrated to France first, then to Canada. The war separated us; I used to see her every day as she would whistle from her kitchen window to ours, a special tune that still rings in my ears. I missed her presence at my graduation and wedding many years later. The war had separated me from her, but she was there at the train station, waiting like a mother. I took a few fishing trips with her husband Jean, a very kind man. They took me to visit all of the French Riviera.

I was then on my way to Paris by train. A good friend of my

father's found me a room in a cheap, shady hotel in the ill-reputed district of Pigalle. There were no elevators to get to the attic room, where I sealed the door and windows at night with heavy-duty chairs. In Paris, I went to see a friend I had made during my short stay a few years prior while a student at the Lycée Honoré de Balzac. The visit was short, and I was on my way to Calais to take the hovercraft to England to stay with my Aunt Sonia in the suburbs of London.

What was the purpose of the trip? My mother probably wanted to get me way from the dangers of the war. Nothing extraordinary happened during the voyage, but I came out of the trip a mature man, ready to face the challenges of tomorrow.

These travel experiences alone at such a young age had probably prepared me to face the new life in America on my own. The second year of residency started on a good note. We were now well integrated into a society that embraced us and our culture. Our culture was the values we picked up from our families, traditions we learned from our people, and beliefs ingrained in our mind, shaping our view of others in relation to ourselves. The cuisine we were used to eating, the taste of fruits and vegetables, even water was different than we were used to, or so we thought. As time passed, the taste slowly changed with the good memories of what it tasted and smelled like remaining. We grew more nostalgic for the good part of our earlier experiences. I never forgot the feeling of the fresh mountain air, but now I better appreciated the beauty of my Garden State. We missed the sunset over the Mediterranean Sea but loved the sunrise over the Atlantic Ocean. We left a noisy city life for a quiet suburban one. The specter of war and fear overshadowed our nostalgia for the country we left as we embraced the peace and serenity of the country we chose. We were happy as we looked forward to our new life.

One day during the second year of my residency, my whole life changed. I remember that morning: I was on duty in the ER and had just picked up a chart, when Ghada came with a radiant smile on her face. In an instant, I became a father. A father—what a beautiful thought.

The next few months, I followed step by step, heartbeat by heartbeat, kick by kick, the birth of Karine. The delivery was a long twenty-two hours, which felt like eternity interrupted by a solemn cry that marked the beginning of another eternity. "It's a girl!" was met with a cry of joy and relief for the poor mother who worked so hard and the lucky dad whose only pain was to hear his brave wife's cry of pain.

She was beautiful, so tiny and sweet. This was my daughter. I escorted her to the nursery. I will never forget that day. A new life was born. It took two people to create this little wonder, and I felt like God might have felt the day he created the world.

I wonder sometimes if God has feelings like we do. He must; otherwise, what is the point of creation? With creation come problems and solutions, worries and wishes. We cannot predict the outcome, which is unique, either good or bad, like a movie script. The sequence of events may already be set in a book called the scriptures. God may have an answer to everything, but then again, where is the element of surprise that breaks the monotony of knowing everything?

We are conscious enough to realize that we are prisoners of a world that we enter through a small hole, and we are not sure whether there is an exit. We lapse into a state where everything is possible and nothing is certain. We spend a lifetime in this prison thinking about this dilemma. Another world perhaps lies ahead, where everything may be perfect, but this one is no prison. There are no mysteries, no worries, no questions to ask, no answers, no hate, and maybe no love—another dimension living outside of time's and space's constraints. Our thought process might be different where black and white do not exist.

Does God feel like us? Does he feel the joy, the happiness, the anger, the compassion, the pride, the love, the hate? Is he human? God created us; these feelings must have crossed his mind. What is the point of eternal life if we don't know what it is like? Again, we might love it or hate it.

Karine was welcomed in our new home by her two grandfathers and my mother. We had made a banner: "Welcome Home, Karine." This moment was captured on videotape, so one day her children can witness the joy of the moment. One day we may be able to capture the whole experience and replay it. We will, however, never be able to change the script. There is only one outcome, one Karine; from an infinite number of possibilities, only one exists, and this is the second certainty in life.

After our medical residency together, Ghada went on to the University of Pennsylvania for three years of subspecialty training in endocrinology, while I went on to the Fox Chase Cancer Center in Philadelphia to pursue training in oncology.

We have gained the respect and admiration of both our patients and colleague physicians alike. We have been named top doctors in the *Philadelphia Magazine* and *New Jersey Monthly Magazine* year after year.

It has been a long journey since we first met on the bench of medical school in Beirut. Ghada has always had the desire to help others, ever since the war days. She had pledged to ease other's suffering and contribute to society in the most positive way she could. She has always had a strong sense of responsibility toward others that she now tries to instill in our daughters' lives.

Bridge of Sighs
Venice, 2006

CHAPTER VI Life and Death

I remember vividly my patient Joe at fifty; he had to face imminent death, and it was during my rotation as an intern on the oncology ward of Cooper Hospital in the spring of 1989. He complained of back pain for a few weeks until his legs gave up on him and he fell. I met him a day later, in his bed on the oncology ward. His face was grief-stricken. He was told that he would not be able to walk again; cancer had just claimed another victim. I tried to comfort him, to tell him about the brighter side of life, to no avail. Joe started to lose weight; he also lost control of his bladder. The worst part was that he had no visitors, no one to lift his spirits. Days passed and pain settled in to crown his misery. He started to lose weight rapidly. At one point he did not recognize me, and I did not recognize him—cancer had changed him so much. A few days later he passed away. I felt so powerless. Sadly, his salvation came from death; his suffering ended.

I decided to become an oncologist, a cancer specialist. Cancer, *saratan* in Arabic, was a word that was banned from the people's language; instead, they called it the Disease. A great number of patients did not know they had just been afflicted with this dreadful disease; it was customary to give the patient a less evil diagnosis.

The whole family would know and think that their beloved one did not know. The patient would not even talk about it since he theoretically did not have it. Things have probably changed since the early nineties. In the land of informed consent, every sinister detail is given to the cancer patient to digest. I had to reconcile the two worlds of the overprotected and overinformed. There were three additional years of training after the three years of internal medicine residency in order to become an oncologist.

Ghada chose the field of endocrinology, the path of the hormones, something she was fascinated by since the first year of medical school. The interview process started again.

We decided to stay in New Jersey and completed our training in Philadelphia. One more test was around the corner: the naturalization. I went to the INS office fully prepared. In a matter of days, I learned American history and memorized all of the amendments to the Constitution but was disappointed to only be asked who the first president of the United States was. I passed with an American flag in my hand.

I started my fellowship with my new beeper glued to my waist day and night for the first six weeks. I had grown to hate the sound of this little black box. A rush of adrenaline surged each time it beeped. Since then, I have always set it on vibrate, a gentler wake-up call. However, this device allowed me to get into the lives of many individuals and get a glimpse of their lives. I was trained as a doctor to try to change the course of their lives; this empowerment comes with moments of glory and others of bitter defeat. There is never one without the other; they are coupled, with eternity as their witness.

Even here we don't get a chance. We have little choice and a decision to make, for good or bad, in sickness and in death. Doctors are a necessity of life; there is no question about it. We are here to help our fellow man in his journey through life. There is nothing nobler than being a guide on the precarious freeway of life. It is always a difficult decision to do no harm, but sometimes it is a necessary evil to get to good. Chemotherapy is such a dreaded evil in the service of good. This toxic tool is what I was trained to use. It is my scalpel.

Every one of my patients has shaped the doctor in me. My teachers added the final touch, and I was ready for a life that would shape other lives. A life helping others—what an ingenious concept. But again, a life destroying another is not so cool. This is a consistent theme in the fabric of our lives.

In the discourse of the origin of disease, this is a necessary evil in the theory of evolution. Or is it merely a punishment as perceived by certain religious groups? If we consider the latter, then what is the purpose of selection? A stronger species, smarter maybe, one that is more ready for phase two of God's plan. Or are we just a tumor that God cannot eradicate, a sort of genetic mutation that went out of control, a defect so disruptive that a universe was created to isolate the problem?

The alternative propositions by religious groups say that man was responsible for many diseases. We created the problem with our actions or even our ancestor's actions. What else is the purpose of disease other than to torture and eventually kill its victim? Some cynical scientists would even propose that it is a medium to open a door to the tree of knowledge, like a survival game feeding the hungry human mind. We must die one day; there is no escape from this reality. Disease is one of the instruments of death. We live longer today than we did thousands of years ago. Disease is in the fabric of life, as if life cannot exist without it. So what is the origin of disease?

The problem with natural selection is that as we become seemingly stronger, so does the disease. It follows evolution like a shadow. We will not outgrow the evolution of disease because it is part of us. For better and for worse, life is intricately linked to disease. So if we accept life, we must deal with its companion. We would not have survived as a human race if we did not try to have an understanding of each disease we are faced with and try to find a cure for each of them. Medicine is a profession that practices the art of healing.

The first rule of a good doctor is one who listens to what

his patient is trying to say. The patient knows more than we sometimes give him credit for. Joseph was in his thirties when I first met him. A malignant lymphoma took over his destiny. He received several courses of chemotherapy that seemed to change his life around. The next year, he got married. Two months later, he called me complaining of a pain in his chest. He was convinced that something wrong was happening, something that he could not explain; he had an eerie feeling of doom. I ordered a CAT scan to alleviate his concern of a cancer recurrence. Hodgkin's disease showed its ugly face again. He struggled once more, to no avail.

The training was so intense; I felt there would be no end to it. During the next nine months, I answered hundreds of calls and made innumerable decisions that shaped the daily lives of each of my patients. It felt like my mind was slipping to another dimension; it was an uncomfortable sense of oppression. I had to perform well every time I was asked; there was no room for mistakes or even hesitation. I so strongly believed that my duty as a doctor was to be flawless that it took me nine long months to realize that it was impossible. The disease is so unpredictable that even the best of the best will be deceived. As we accept life and its companion diseases, we must equally accept our failures as we take pride in our successes. During moments of despair, we wish we could be God but realize we are only human.

On one snowy day in February 1994, the joy of parenthood came again. The baby kicked very hard during pregnancy, so we thought it was a boy. The night before Joelle was born, we had gone to the Philadelphia Orchestra to listen to the music of Wagner. After a stunning performance of *Tannhauser* and *Die Walkure*, a big kick that ruptured the membranes sent us rushing to Pennsylvania Hospital. There were twelve hours of intense labor, with a sudden drop of Ghada's blood pressure. My heart was racing, and my numb mind was suddenly awakened by a cry: "It's a girl!" I broke into tears of joy for the birth of Joelle.

I accompanied her on her first trip away from her mother, to the nursery. She was beautiful. She was a little jaundiced, too; I took her to get a blood test. She got her innocent little heel stuck. She cried and cried, and my heart wanted to stop. Within a few days, the jaundice faded away, leaving a cute, healthy pinkish color.

Karine welcomed her sister with open arms. It is hard to imagine what went on in her three-year-old mind when she first saw her.

Life went on. After finishing our training in Philadelphia, we both came back to the city of Camden. We each got an appointment as assistant professor of medicine at the University of Medicine of New Jersey. Over the next few years, between 1994 and 2000, I had the privilege to care for a lot of patients. Although they all taught me many lessons of life and death, some made a lasting impression.

One of my first patients was Mr. M; he was a teacher who had just retired. His cough betrayed the cancer that was in his lungs. He always had a smile on his face and a funny joke to tell. That year, Ghada was nominated as a top doctor in the Delaware valley. Her picture was in the *Philadelphia Magazine*. Mr. M said to me, with a candid smile on his face, "When are you going to be in that magazine?" He said this just to let me know how he appreciated me. The chemotherapy was not successful. His lung cancer spread, but he always kept his sense of humor. During his last days, he wanted to come to see me in the office. He was too weak to travel. I showed up at his house. His son greeted me by telling me he thought Dr. Welby was fictional. Doctors have stopped making home visits for the most part. He was grateful that I could come. He felt better just seeing me. I have made a few house calls since then; the odd part is that I was as happy to see them as they were to see me.

Albert was in his thirties when I took care of him. He was a good friend and a brilliant doctor. One day he felt dizzy. One thing led to another; he was diagnosed with metastatic cancer that had spread from his bones to his brain. I saw him in the intensive care unit with a drain coming from his brain and an intravenous catheter in each arm. His pathology was sent to the best doctors to determine the origin of his cancer. I called on national and international experts. The picture was grim. Albert received one cycle of chemotherapy and brain irradiation in an attempt to control the fire that was consuming him. A fungal infection spread throughout his body and he lapsed in a coma. We tried to resuscitate him, but his hour had come. I hugged his sister; no words could express my distress. I could not save my friend. I went to my car and cried.

When I met Barbara in my office, she was scared. She was just diagnosed with lung cancer that had spread to the liver. She knew what that meant and said, "I put my life in God's hands, and I trust you will help me." She was treated with chemotherapy for six months, after which her cancer disappeared. She had seen her children grow and hugged her first grandchild. She celebrated the new millennium; she is still alive today.

Margaret was in her seventies when she was diagnosed with lymphoma. She had stoically taken care of her husband a few months prior. He was seriously ill; she was always at his bedside, and that's where we met. She wanted to find out why he became so critically ill so fast. She gave me the key to the puzzle; I listened to her and valued her input. My knowledge and her insight led to the discovery of a rare condition from which he had suffered. He recovered without sequela. She was so dedicated to him that she blocked all the pain she herself had suffered from during those long months. She prioritized his well-being over hers. She is my hero.

Margaret received chemotherapy, which helped her for a very short period of time, after which her condition deteriorated very fast. As I entered her room, she had an angelic smile on her face. She said to me her last words, which still resonate in my ears today: "You're a doll. Thank you." She died few hours later. It was like I had lost a mother.

I treated Rita for metastatic lung cancer for about two years. The last day I saw her, she was lying in her hospital bed. I calmly tried to explain her condition when she suddenly interrupted me and said in a very peaceful voice, "My mother is here. She came to take me with her."

I turned around to see who was there, but I saw no one. Her mother had died a few years ago. She saw her, but I felt her presence. It is hard to put into words what had happened that instant. I found myself at the crossroad of two worlds. A few hours later, her husband informed me that she had passed away, with a smile on her face.

I always tried to plan treatment to meet certain milestones that my patients set for themselves, whether it was the wedding of Mr. C's daughter or Joe's fiftieth anniversary, or the birth of Mrs. G's grandchild, or the miraculous birth of Susan's son, Noah. I did not always succeed. Anthony passed away before he could witness the birth of his grandson Anthony. Through his name, the memory of a good man was resurrected. Mr. C was not able walk his daughter down the aisle, but the night before he passed, he gathered all his strength to attend her engagement party and give his blessings.

The story of Bob is one that defies death. It started more than four years ago. Bob was a very active man, full of life. Overnight, his life changed; he was diagnosed with acute leukemia. After the first course of intensive chemotherapy, the malignant cells peaked through his skin while he was receiving another course of therapy. This is usually an ominous sign of doom. A new treatment became available, and his disease went into remission. A bone marrow transplant was considered, but there were no matched donor. Four months later, his leukemia was back. He received another round of therapy, complicated by shaking chills and high fever. He responded well again. At that time, he was planning a trip to the old country of Italy. His son was also getting engaged, and the wedding set for April 29, 2005.

Six weeks before the trip of a lifetime, the malignant cells peeked through his skin again. I had to perform another bone marrow biopsy, Bob's tenth one in the past fifteen months. We tried to control his disease with radiation to minimize side effects and allow him to still go on his trip. Two weeks later and only a few days before his trip, the disease struck again, weakening his body. He was back in the hospital. I searched intensively for the most efficient treatment to get him in remission and maintain it for more than seven months, to get him to the most important day of his life, the wedding of his son. He received another course of intensive chemotherapy for the next five weeks. With a weakened immune system, he was at the mercy of a number of bacteria and fungi ready to overcome him. He came out weakened but in remission, thanks to several antibiotics and many transfusions. His sense of humor never faded. He went on to receive another course of chemotherapy to ensure that his remission would be more likely to outlast the wedding date.

There was of course no guarantee that he would survive; the odds were always against him. After another long hospitalization, Bob emerged in remission only a few months prior to the most important day of his life. We were sitting in the office just a couple weeks before the wedding, and I received a personal invitation to attend. A very emotional father walked his daughter-in-law down the aisle—her own father had passed away a few years prior after another battle with cancer—toward his equally emotional son. When Bob saw me, he hugged and thanked me. I felt that, that day, together, we defeated the odds, and in the end, all the years of suffering were worth every second of that day. That night I was introduced to his entire family. I sat at the family table and received so many thanks that the memory of them would last me a lifetime. After the wedding, Bob and Janet went on their trip to my favorite place, Italy.

Life was too beautiful. The leukemia returned. One month of

intensive chemotherapy sent the blast away only to return a few weeks after, but this time a virulent strain of a bacterium called Klebsiella sent a shock wave as strong as a tsunami. When I came to visit him on December 10, 2005, I was not able to recognize him. I hugged his wife and said farewell to a very dear friend. The next morning, as I was about to kneel during church service, my cell phone vibrated to the tune of Mozart's *Requiem* and I knew then that Bob had passed away to the other side.

Jill, My Mother, 1950

Chapter VII My Heritage

My father, Daniel, passed away on March 17, 2001. That day, I lost my link to my ancestors and part of my life. My father was born many moons ago, at the end of the First World War, in Lebanon. His father, Alexandre, whom I have been named after, was a great lawyer in Alexandria, Egypt. I never met my grandfather; he passed away a year before my birth. My father told me that he was very smart. He was also an art collector and a horse race fan. He was involved in high-profile cases. He died a few months after a mysterious car accident. His wife, Marie, died a few years before, after a long battle with breast cancer. I can imagine now the struggle they faced in the dark ages of oncology, when surgery was primitive, radiation therapy was experimental, and chemotherapy was nonexistent. They went from one alternative medicine to another, from a local doctor to a European one. She died one day on Easter; she took her last breath in the arms of her son, my father. That was a snapshot he never forgot.

My father had a brother and two sisters. The youngest was called Adrienne. *Reine* was the French word for "queen." She was a beauty who was struck with a terrible illness. She was about to be married, when a Western surgeon decided to remove part of her brain—a lobotomy, as we call it. During the World War II air raids on Egypt, the teenaged queen's nervous system broke down.

She behaved strangely enough to warrant this terrible infliction that she had to live with for the rest of her life.

My grandparents sought the best medical opinions in the world. She was treated with words, pills, and electric shocks, until she faced the most mutilating of all treatments, a frontal lobotomy. All of my grandfather's savings went up in flames; the family's attention was focused on the illnesses of the two dearest women of the family.

Tina is what I called my uncle; he was justly named after the first Christian martyr Etienne. In his teenage years, he played every sport, courted every beauty queen, and dropped out of school. He had a good life. He made a promise to his mother on her deathbed, which he honored until the day he died, that he would take care of his sick sister. Life was tough after this; he had no inheritance since everything was spent on medical care. He always took care of my aunt; he treated her like his daughter. He never married. They lived in a small apartment in Tayoune, a suburb that turned to a front line during the war, a very dangerous place to live. They lived the majority of the war in their sister's house a few steps away from yet another hot front line. Bikfaya was their ultimate refuge until a highway project destroyed their last refuge. It was sad to see the family house brought down stone by stone, brick by brick. A piece of the land with four guardian trees remained as a testimony to our past.

When my aunt died, Tina never stopped talking to her, as if she hadn't died. He would suddenly stop our telephone conversation to continue the argument he had with his sister. He loved her so much; he could not bear the idea that she was gone.

He passed away just a year after her death. He sacrificed his life to care for his sister. He is my hero.

My uncle Etienne managed to be the best tennis teacher I have known. He made a living teaching tennis and gave free lessons to those who could not afford it. He wanted everyone to be passionate about his favorite sport.

I best enjoyed his bedtime stories, most of which were about his adventures during his teenage years. He used to give me a modest weekly allowance. He was not rich by any means, but he gave everything he had to his loved ones.

Bikfaya was his paradise. The village was the birthplace of my family and incidentally of two of Lebanon's controversial presidents: Bashir and Amine Gemayel. Bikfaya is a quiet village sitting on top of Mount Lebanon. A few spring water sources scattered around the outskirts of the village attracted those thirsty for water as well as those thirsty for love. Each source attracted a different crowd; each had a different taste of water blending with the soil through which it traveled and the mountain air it breathed.

Naas was my favorite one, set in a forest of pines laid on a reddish soil at the top of the mountain. A winding, narrow road flanked by majestic pines led to the source. The water was cold with a zest of pine. Villagers and visitors came to this site charged with empty gallons, to capture the precious liquid. In the summer, the place was packed with tourists staying at nearby hotels.

Ashoush was my uncle's favorite; he made daily trips to this sanctuary, perhaps looking for someone or to meet someone. He would just sit, drink the spring water, and forget his daily pain. This source was hidden at the feet of the mount that led to Naas, in a cul-de-sac surrounded by high peaks. Here the water flowed abundantly from multiple gorges, making all kinds of sounds. Once you sat there, the sound of water played an enchanting symphony with the wind blowing through the trees and the mountain echoing the music like a choir.

Our third favorite source was a small one in Bhersaf, at the edge of the village. We would climb together, about a few hundred steps from our house. We stopped frequently along the way to take a look back at the beautiful natural landscape of the mountains and valleys, sigh as if one day we would never see it again, and continue on our journey. He would tell me stories along the way about how it was when he was my age. He would pick a plant, rub it between his fingers, and make me smell the treasured perfumes hidden in our path, never to forget his favorite place on earth. Along the way, the smell of freshly baked bread mixed with the fresh air of the mountain was a prelude to the taste of the water.

On the way back down to the house was an exhilarating downward sequence of steep steps, sharp turns, and flat trails leading to our house. The house was made of carved grayish stones standing two stories high from the main highway, with a brick red roof. The garden was wild. There were three large steps made of stone that continued up to the top of the mount. There were four trees that stood tall and proud of their fruits. A green olive tree sat at the southern entrance of the house. Two fig trees, a white and a purple one, flanked the olive tree to the west entrance. A pistachio tree secured the northern entrance to the house.

The house was built in the late nineteenth century by my great-grandfather. There were three rooms on each floor. I rarely ventured to the first floor. It had been abandoned since the early twentieth century, and an old woman struck with a stroke, a distant relative, lived there part of her miserable life. My childhood image of her was that of a witch dressed in black, with long tangled white hair, crooked fingers, and a paralyzed arm. I grew up to know her simple mind. She was an outcast to her own family; she lived a lonely life. She never hurt a soul. She was the tenant of the run-down first floor.

The second floor was our summer refuge from the heat of the city. A big green door opened to the living room, a square room flanked by the bedroom to the north and the kitchen and bathroom to the south. Another green door, with an arch window atop, opened to the balcony and a majestic view to the surrounding Mount Lebanon, the valley, and a glimpse of the Mediterranean Sea.

Once a year before the war started, during the summer, a parade of flower-decorated cars rolled through the main street in the center of the village, commemorating the beauty of nature. Both sides of the street were packed with villagers and visitors who attended this yearly event. My father would lift me on his shoulder to take a glimpse at the cars decorated with flowers. My uncle would treat me to a special ice cream.

My father courted my mother for seven years before they got married. My grandfather wanted him to become a lawyer; he never did. He took a job at IBM selling typewriters. Then he moved up the corporate ladder to a managerial position. He always warned me against being involved in political parties. I do not remember any other serious father-to-son conversation we had. My mother, Gilberte, was the most beautiful woman my father had ever met. She had two sisters, Sylvie and Sonia, and twin brothers, Georges and Robert. I later learned that she had another brother who died of some infectious disease at a very young age.

Her father, Kamel, had a soap factory; he lost the business after World War II. My mother and her sisters started to work at a very young age. They supported the family, and with her savings, she bought a few books. Her passion for reading stayed with her.

One sister, Sonia, married a British officer, Bill Downhill, and they lived in England. Her eldest sister, Sylvie, married an Italian doctor, Tony Piazza; they lived in Venice. Her twin brothers moved to America when I was born. Robert married and moved to California. George took care of my grandmother Georgette.

Uncle George was also my chosen godfather; however, the church denied me that right because he was Orthodox and I was Maronite. They are similar Christian faiths but there are different church rules and regulations. George and my mother were the driving forces that paved the way to my coming to this land of opportunity. They both had a vision of a better future for me, for which I will always be grateful. George is a generous and kind person, who started cleaning restrooms for a living before establishing himself as a very successful real estate broker. He married Araxie, a wonderful young Armenian who had just emigrated from Lebanon. Together they sheltered many immigrant couples and never asked anything in return—such a rare gift. My wife, Ghada, and I were blessed to be among those lucky couples who went on to have a successful life in this new land.

My mother worked in a travel agency of Air Liban to get free airline tickets to visit her family abroad. She never wanted to miss a minute in the lives of her family, which had spread around the globe. She worked there until my coming into this world; she later stayed home to take care of my brother and me. My parents were always a happy couple.

My father survived a car bomb that nailed a few pieces of glass shrapnel into his back. A few years later, while changing a flat tire, a young man crashed his motorcycle into his head; he survived that one, too. His last challenge was cancer. I remembered that day vividly, as if it was today. He told me, "My pill is getting stuck in my throat." I looked into his throat; the ugly face of cancer looked back at me. There was large tonsil tumor and a pill stuck between its pillars. After an intense chemotherapy and radiotherapy course, the tumor retreated for a year.

I was on the phone that day when he told me that his shoulder itched; I remember the sight of cancer that crawled from under his shoulder skin and through his back. I knew then that I would lose my father very soon. He accepted his fate with great dignity. He received more treatment, which maintained a good quality of life until the last month of his life. He told me then, "You have done enough for me; my hour has come." That month we also prepared to move to our new home in Moorestown. I can still see him entering the foyer of the new home with a cane supporting his frail body. He took a quick glance around and then hugged and kissed me, wishing me all the good luck. Within a few days he went from using the cane to using the walker, from talking to mumbling. He quickly lapsed into a coma. Over the next few days I changed him and bathed him like he once changed and bathed me. I said good-bye. Peace be with you, Dad.

My father passed away on the first St. Patrick's Day of the third millennium. A mass was celebrated at Saint Thomas More Church. A eulogy followed. I stood by the coffin and said, "The first thing my father would have said is thank you all for coming. He was a good man. He was a good friend to many who trusted him. They have called from all over the world to pay their respects to the friend who helped them when they needed help, and he was a man of his word. He was a hard worker who worked all his life to provide for his family. He risked his life to go to work under the threat of bombs, snipers, and kidnappers. His co-workers always knew they could rely on him.

"He was a good uncle to his nephew and niece; he was like a father to them when their father passed away a few years ago. He was a good brother to his baby sister. They helped each other care for their sister throughout her lifelong illness. His mother died in his arms some forty years ago during the same month of March. She also struggled with cancer.

"God was good to him; he put him in the path of a wonderful woman." A moment of strong emotion silenced my voice for an instant.

"He loved and cherished her every moment of his life. In sickness and in health, in richness and in poorness, in wartime and in peacetime, even death could not set them apart.

"Joelle, six years of age at the time, told me the day he died, 'Pappy, do you know the best thing Jeddo (the name she called her grandfather) ever did? It was to have had you and your brother Pierre.'" My voice was fading, as I tried to control my emotions.

"He shaped our lives and led us in the right path. He protected us during the war and gave us the best education we could get. We made him proud. Thank you, Dad." I laid my hand on his coffin.

"He would have reminded me of his two daughters, whom he loved and respected. He was a good father-in-law. He helped raise and educate their children.

"Last but not least, he was a wonderful grandfather to four grandchildren: Thomas and Philippe in Lebanon, and Karine and Joelle here in America. He was there when they were born; he helped in any way he could to raise them like he raised us.

"He spent his retirement with his grandchildren, helping in every way he could to give them a better life. The last smile I saw on my father's face was the day my daughter came to his room. As if all the suffering stopped for an instant, a smile lit up his face as if he just saw the sunshine of his life.

"Jeddo loves you very much."

My Angels
St. Thomas, Virgin Islands, 1995

Chapter VIII Interview with God

As I left my father in his last resting place in Colestown Cemetery in Cherry Hill, New Jersey, I remembered when I was growing up, leaving church with my father on Sundays. The flashback of the sound of the church bell, the heartwarming sound of the choir, and the scent of incense that filled the air came rushing back. I missed listening to the incantation in Aramaic to the sound of "Qadishat Aloho, Qadishat Haylthono, Qadishat lo MoyouTHo, eTHraHam al'ain."[7]

It brought back a sense of mystique, mixed with the sounds and sights of fireworks on religious holidays during the summer. I missed praying with my dad. I hoped that my prayers would get the attention of God and that one day my monologue would be answered and would change to a dialogue.

When I first wrote this chapter, I asked God my questions, and God answered. Something was wrong because I was writing my words in God's name in a manner similar to all of the interpreters of Holy Scriptures, regardless of their religious affiliation.

I just put down the words that made sense to me, not the words that made sense to everyone.

So I decided to rewrite this chapter in the format of a prayer, with the hope of getting my questions answered.

My God, who are you?

My God, who am I?

When I look at your creation, I see you, God.

When your creation looks at me, who will they see?

Adam was faced with two choices.

If I were Adam, what choice would I have to make?

"You shall not kill" is your command.

Why in your name are so many wars fought?

Angela, mother of two, died today after a six-year battle with cancer.

Cancer, sickness, warfare, illness.

Why all this suffering?

What is our crime?

Why did you create me without the answer to every question?

Why don't you teach me like I teach my children?

Perhaps I should stop asking why.

I believe there is only one message: to love each other.

I believe there is only one God.

I believe.

Amen.

Memories of the Past
Temple of Bacchus
Baalbek, 1996

CHAPTER IX The Nightmare Returns

Childhood memories were fading away, like a sandcastle on a beach; memories of the war were starting to fade, too. I never thought when I started writing this book that I would end it with another dream.

"The Nightmare Returns" is a title worthy of a Hollywood movie that would be a hit at the box office.

I woke up scared and shaky; I had just had another nightmare. I was almost forty. I vividly remember that dream. The dream was short; it felt like a flashback. The emotions were high, and fear was at its center. First, a building appeared, in flames like an inferno. Next I became aware of an evil figure circling the building. That figure soon looked me in the eye. I stopped being a spectator and became the prey. I wanted to wake up. As I became aware that it was only a dream, I moaned and groaned, but my voice was muted, and my fear grew stronger as I saw no escape from the evil-looking creature that was devouring me with its eyes. I suddenly woke up very disturbed and restless. I looked at the time it was four o'clock on the morning of the September 11, 2001.

I fell back asleep reluctantly. Later that morning, as I was sitting in a chair in the chemotherapy infusion center, discussing the side effects of chemotherapy with David, who was diagnosed with lymphoma, I watched a surrealistic image on the television that sent shivers down my spine: two planes had just hit the two towers of the World Trade Center. The evil face of war had struck again, this time in the land of freedom and security, in my safe haven.

I stopped for a minute and wanted to wake up from my dream, but I could not; this one was real.

I thought I had found a sanctuary in which to raise my children. This was a rude awakening that there is no sanctuary or safe haven on earth.

The memories of the war rushed back: the vision of the burning buildings, the screams of the victims crying for help, the despair of the rescuers, the pain of the wounded, the anguish of the mothers, and the suffocating smell of smoke and gunpowder.

I had the unbearable realization that thousands of men and women died in that instant, and thousands of families lost a father or mother, a brother or a sister, a son or a daughter. This was not an act of God or nature; this was an evil, manmade act.

There is no point in asking why, because there is no answer that would justify the murder of the innocents.

Action and reaction ensued. The war ignited, in Afghanistan first and then Iraq. This cycle has to end, or maybe it is part of the cycle of life. History is full of stories of wars, from the slaying of Cain to the mass murder of 9/11. There is no stopping the war machine, as if history cannot live without it.

War is an unfortunate fact of life. People who fight for or against it become victims of its wrath. War is fueled by men's hatred of other men, by the desire to dominate and feel powerful, by the need to quell anger. War is sometimes the work of a madman whose only pleasure is to witness destruction, like a killer watching his victim suffer and die.

Can war be eradicated? No.

We have made progress through the ages to control and regulate war. It has become a science, one that can generate discoveries that on occasion make our lives better. The knowledge of medicine, engineering, and laws have all benefited from the death of the innocents. I sometimes tell my students the story of nitrogen mustard, which was manufactured as a powerful chemical weapon with the sole purpose of killing more men during World War II. A ship carrying a load of this compound was destined to reach the Allied forces when it came under attack by the German air force. The ship sunk, leaking the chemical, which poisoned some of the crew members. The soldiers who initially survived the incident died two weeks later from severe infection.

Doctors Alfred Gillman and Louis S. Goodman discovered that nitrogen mustard led to a state of deficiency of the immune system that resulted from the destruction of white blood cells. This later became one of the first successful chemotherapy agents in the fight against cancer.[8]

However, the vast majority of discoveries that benefited us were born from an idea to heal rather than to kill.

Money and power is a dangerous combination that has fueled many wars. Only a few wise men in power have resisted its intoxicating effect. President Eisenhower, in his farewell address to the nation on January 17, 1961, warned us about the industrial machinery of war:

"In the councils of government, we must guard against the acquisition of unwarranted influence, whether sought or unsought, by the military industrial complex. The potential for the disastrous rise of misplaced power exists and will persist. We must never let the weight of this combination endanger our liberties or democratic processes. We should take nothing for granted. Only an alert and knowledgeable citizenry can compel the proper meshing of the huge industrial and military machinery of defense with our peaceful methods and goals, so that security and liberty may prosper together."[9]

Do I have a solution? I realize that war cannot be eradicated, as it is woven in the fabric of life as we continue to support the development of weapons and the art of killing. War is about defending ideology, honor, land, and liberty, but it is also about the less-than-noble intentions of conquering, enslaving, stealing, and exterminating.

In the first four decades of my life, I have witnessed more than ten wars: the Lebanese Civil War, at least three Israeli-Arab wars, the Serbian War, Somalia, Darfur, Rwanda, Afghanistan, and Iraq. Following the attack on September 11, the war in Afghanistan was an example of a war driven by noble ideas of defending freedom and attempting to stop the rise of terrorism. On the other hand, in the war against Iraq, noble ideas were magnified based on the presence of weapons of mass destruction that were never found, which in the context of fighting terrorism, was just enough to overlook other intentions. So many died, so many suffered, so many were lost, and yet no one has won.

The decision to go to war is too large of a responsibility to fall on a few whose names history will remember while time blurs the names of the many casualties of war.

We cannot continue to support dictators, religious fanatics, and extremists in the name of our national interest. We are only solidifying the belief that we don't care.

We supported Saddam Hussein as a ruthless dictator; then we hanged him decades later for crimes against humanity. We supported Osama Bin Laden, who in turn masterminded, decades later, the killings of September 11. To continue on the same path will only lead to a continuum of world conflict, fueling many wars to come.

I witnessed the war in Lebanon live on my street. I witnessed many other wars on television in the comfort of my home. I could not stop the war that consumed my adolescence or any other that consumed so many lives. I can only write and hope that war, like diseases, can sometimes be prevented.

Is there an end to the Israeli-Palestinian conflict? This is an everlasting conflict in the history of humanity. This conflict fueled the civil war in Lebanon by displacing a large portion of the Palestinian population, who found refuge in Lebanon. They came with their weapons, which ultimately targeted my childhood neighborhood during the war.[10]

The conflict may have started with the clash of David and

Goliath. The stone throwing of the modern age conflict is reminiscent of the Old Testament. The message that the stone portrays is simple: it's a piece of land that is worth dying for, and it's the most precious possession of all. We can build our homes with it. It provides protection, security, and peace. It is amazing how a minority's wish on either side could galvanize a larger number to join in the conflict and perpetuate the cycle of violence.

Is it possible for David and Goliath to come together in an attempt to end the conflict? They want the same peace on the same piece of land. This would certainly make a nice story worthy of being told for the next millennium to come and would perhaps help future generations put an end to endless conflict.

What is the first step of this reconciliation? Perhaps a handshake would be a good start. A handshake would get them close enough to feel that they are both human, they both have families. The best part of attending church services is the time when everyone gives peace to each other in the form of a handshake. It's a rare occasion to stop and look your neighbor in the eye and then exchange a smile and a handshake and add the final touch, uttering a few words: "Peace be with you." The overall effect is so appeasing—a true flavor of peace.

The traditional agreement is finalized by both parties signing a document. Traditionally, delegates of both parties come up with the principal elements of the agreement. Several of these agreements have been signed already. So what's the problem? Why isn't it working?

The short answer is that not everyone shared the views of the delegates, and a small but powerful group was able to take advantage of these different views and amplify the schism between the two communities with a grain of salt. Previous failures were due to a lack of vision.

How, then, can we build a solid agreement? Let's start building a home for this agreement. To build the House of Peace, *Beit El Salam* or *Beit Shalom*, would require the efforts of both communities. The house will be built of stones provided by every village and town from both communities. Stones of hate will be transformed into stones of love. The location will be on a prime piece of land, far from the cities and towns, with a view of the sea and mountains. The builders, architects, engineers, interior designers, artists, plumbers, electricians, carpenters, gardeners, painters, and roofers will be provided by both communities, to work together designing and building the house of both communities' dream of peace. In the garden of the house, trees will be planted from every community in the land; side by side the trees will grow and flower.

A large playground designed by the children of the same God will be the centerpiece of peace. Innocence will be restored by the sound of children playing just to have fun.

The political leaders will focus on making compromises. Politicians will compromise in the best interest of their children rather their own quest for power and fame. The religious leaders will try to preach tolerance; this should be easy since they believe in the same God, even the same prophets like Abraham.

Once the house is built, the leaders of both communities will sign the agreement of everlasting peace in the hall of the house.

This sounds so simple that it could actually work, so simple that no one would believe it could work.

In order to heal, a large wound needs stitches to hold the two edges together for a little while until both parts of the wound realize that together the wound would heal faster.

A signature on a piece of paper is too fragile in the Middle East to sustain the pressure of differences between the communities. A signature, a handshake, a house, a garden, a playground, and the uttering of just a few words—no more war, please—should create the stitching effect that would hold peace together.

Light at the End of the Tunnel
The Blue Grotto
Capri, 2005

Chapter X Light at the End of the Tunnel

I left my homeland, my past, and my childhood, and now all I have left are my memories of what it was like. When I look back at the path I walked, I wonder how I survived, who I lost, and what my life could have been if war had never happened. I embrace this life, with all its joy and pain. I have no regrets.

If I have to make a wish for the next years of my life and the lives of my children, I wish that war becomes history that will not repeat itself, that diplomacy will always resolve conflicts.

Today, August 3, 2008, there is a war in Iraq and one in Afghanistan, and there is still an unresolved conflict in the Middle East and in many parts of the world. By the time this book gets published, I will have voted for the next president of the United States of America. The burden of leadership of the next president is to foremost restore peace in the world; it will be a difficult but not impossible task.

I cannot stop the war; I can only write and hope that my message is received by the one who will hold the power to bring an end to the worst manmade disaster—war.

I see the light at the end of the tunnel. I don't know if I will be writing the next chapter; perhaps one of you will be able to write what it is like to live in a world with no more wars.

Acknowledgments

I would like to thank my wife, Ghada, for all her love and support; she is my muse and my inspiration for this book. A special thanks to my daughters, Karine and especially Joelle, who spent hours correcting and editing.

I am ever grateful to my mother and father for all their support, guidance, and unconditional love. I am grateful as well to my wife's family, especially Laure and Nicolas, who embraced me and loved me as their own son. I would like to especially thank my uncle George Naufal and his wife Araxie, who helped me get a head start in this land of opportunity.

I am indebted to all my teachers, especially Dr. Edward Viner, as well as to all my patients, who taught me so much about life.

Bibliography

Bosworth, A. B. *Conquest and Empire: The Reign of Alexander the Great.* Cambridge: Cambridge University Press, 1988

Churchill, Charles Henry. *The Druzes and the Maronites under the Turkish Rule from 1840 to 1860.* New York: Arno Press, 1973.

Cleveland, William L.*A History of the Modern Middle East: Second Edition.* Boulder: Westview Press, 2000.

Collelo, Thomas. *Lebanon: A Country Study/* Federal Research Division, Library of Congress. Washington DC: U.S. G.P.O., 1989

Eisenhower, Dwight D. *Public Papers of the Presidents, Dwight D. Eisenhower.* Washington DC: Government Printing Office, 1961.

Goodman, Louis S. 1984.Landmark article Sept. 21, 1946: Nitrogen mustard therapy. Use of methyl-bis (beta-chloroethyl) amine hydrochloride and tris (beta-chloroethyl) amine hydrochloride for Hodgkin's disease, lymphosarcoma, leukemia and certain allied, and miscellaneous disorders. JAMA 251:2255-2261

Hansen, William. *Handbook of Classical Mythology.* Santa Barbara: ABC-CLIO, 2004.

King, Archdal. *The Rites of Eastern Christendom*: Gorgias Press LLC, 2007

Salibi, Kamal Suleiman. *A House of Many Mansions: The History of Lebanon Reconsidered.* Los Angeles: University of California Press, 1988.

Scarre, Chris. *The Penguin Historical Atlas of Ancient Rome.* London: Penguin Books, 1995.

Endnotes

1 Hansen, *Handbook of Classical Mythology,*

2 Collelo, *Lebanon : A Country Study,*

3 Bosworth, *Conquest and Empire: The Reign of Alexander the Great,*

4 Scarre, *The Penguin Historical Atlas of Ancient Rome,*

5 Salibi, *A House of Many Mansions: The History of Lebanon Reconsidered,*

6 Churchill, *The Druzes and the Maronites under the Turkish Rule from 1840 to 1860,* 23.

7 King, *The Rites of Eastern Christendom,*

8 Goodman, "Nitrogen Mustard Therapy," JAMA 251:2255–61.

9 Eisenhower, *Public Papers of the Presidents,* 1035–40.

10 Cleveland, *History of the Modern Middle East: Second Edition,*

Dad, Mom and Uncle Georges, 1949

Scars of War, Lebanon, 1981

Scars of War, Lebanon, 1981

More Scars of War, Lebanon, 1981

More Scars of War, Lebanon, 1981

My Neighborhood during the War, Lebanon, 1981

My Neighborhood during the War, Lebanon, 1981

My Family and I, Bikfaya,1964

Printed in the United States
140667LV00003B/56/P